40 STUDIES FOR CLARINET

C. ROSE

Book I
Book II

Published in 2019 by Allegro Editions

40 Studies for Clarinet [Cmplt]
ISBN: 978-1-9748-9952-4 (paperback)

Cover design by Kaitlyn Whitaker

Cover image: "Close Up Detail of a Woodwind Clarinet"
by Mark Yuill, courtesy of Shutterstock;
"Music Sheet" by Danielo, courtesy of Shutterstock

ALLEGRO
EDITIONS

40
STUDIES
FOR
CLARINET

Book I

40 STUDIES
for
CLARINET.

BOOK I.

arr. by C. ROSE.

Moderato. 𝅗𝅥 = 96.
Nº 2.
dolcissimo

Moderato. ♩=96.
Nº 3.

Allegro. 𝅗𝅥 = 144.
Nº 4.
tr
Presto

Allegro. 𝅗𝅥 = 126.

No. 5.

Moderato. ♩ = 92.
Nº 6.
léger

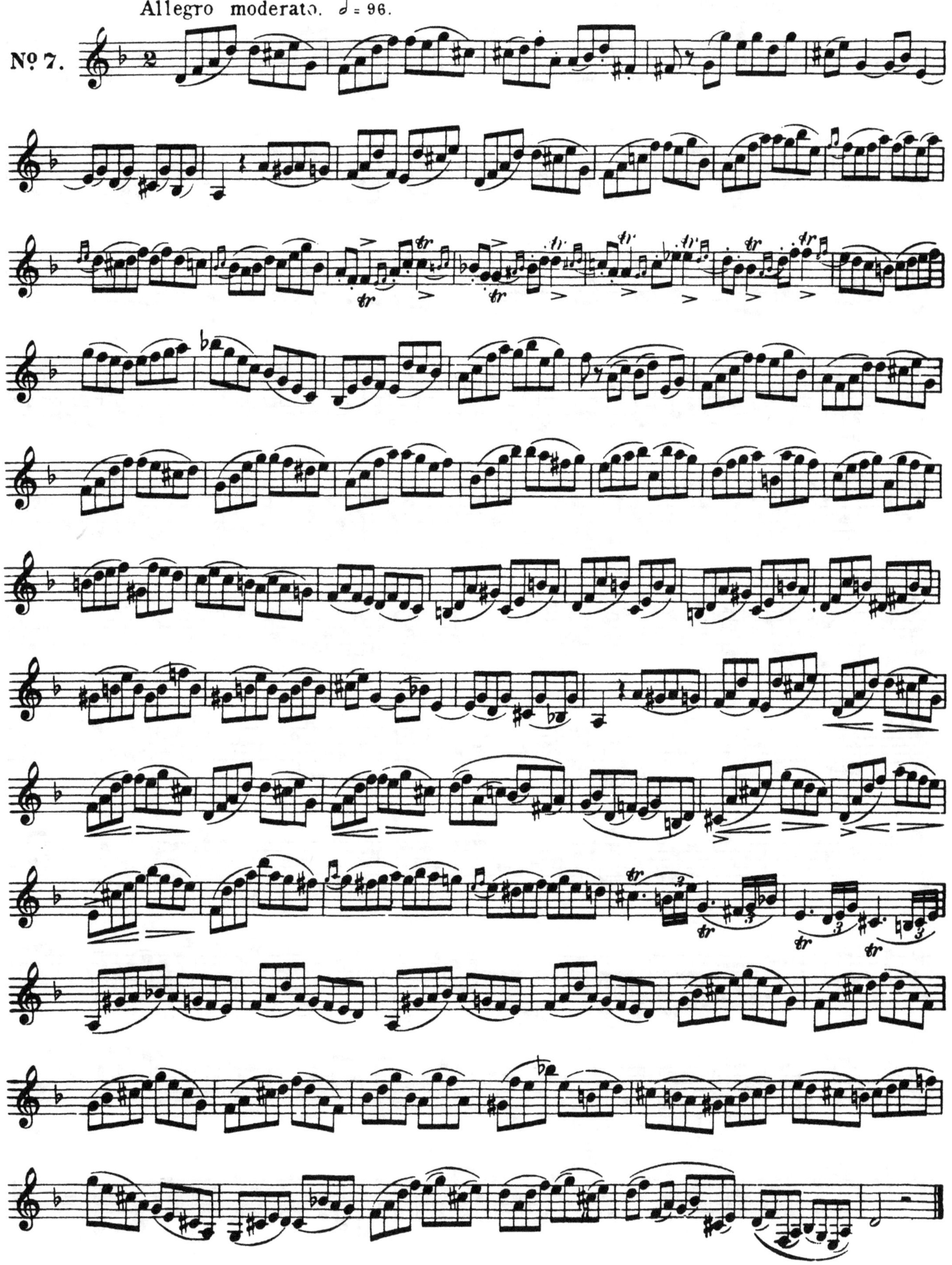
Allegro moderato. 𝅗𝅥 = 96.
Nº 7.
tr

Allegro moderato. ♩ = 116.

Nº 8.

Moderato. ♩= 92.
Nº 9.
p
tr
tr

Allegro. 𝅗𝅥 = 126.
Nº 10.
p très légerement

p
f

Allegretto. ♩. = 76.
Nº 11.

Allegretto. ♩.=72.
Nº 12.
p
cresc.
poco
f
p
cresc.
f
p
cresc.
f
p
cresc.
poco
a
poco
f

Adagio. ♩ = 69.
Nº 13.
pathetique
f
e sostenuto
largement
mf
dolce.
p
mf
p
mf
p
animez
cresc.
Andante con moto. ♩ = 88.
dim.
pp
p
f
p
f
rit.
dim.
pp
pp
p
dolcissimo
poco rit.
ppp

Allegro moderato. ♩ 112.
Nº 14.
dolce.
mf
f
p

Allegro moderato. ♩=108.
Nº 15.
p

Moderato. ♩ = 104.
Nº 16.
f
tr
sf

Allegretto. ♩ = 96.
Nº 17.

tr
tr
tr
tr

Adagio. ♩ = 48.
Nº 18.
espressivo
p
tr
mf
poco f
tr
p
mf
cresc.
f
dim. rit.
tr
pp
p
cresc.
tr
p
mf
cresc
rit.
tr
pp

Moderato. 𝅗𝅥 = 104.

№ 19.

Polonaise. ♩= 104.
Nº 20.
tr
p
f
sfp
mf
cresc - - - poco f
dim.

40
STUDIES
FOR
CLARINET

Book II

40 STUDIES
for
CLARINET.

BOOK II.

arr. by C. ROSE.

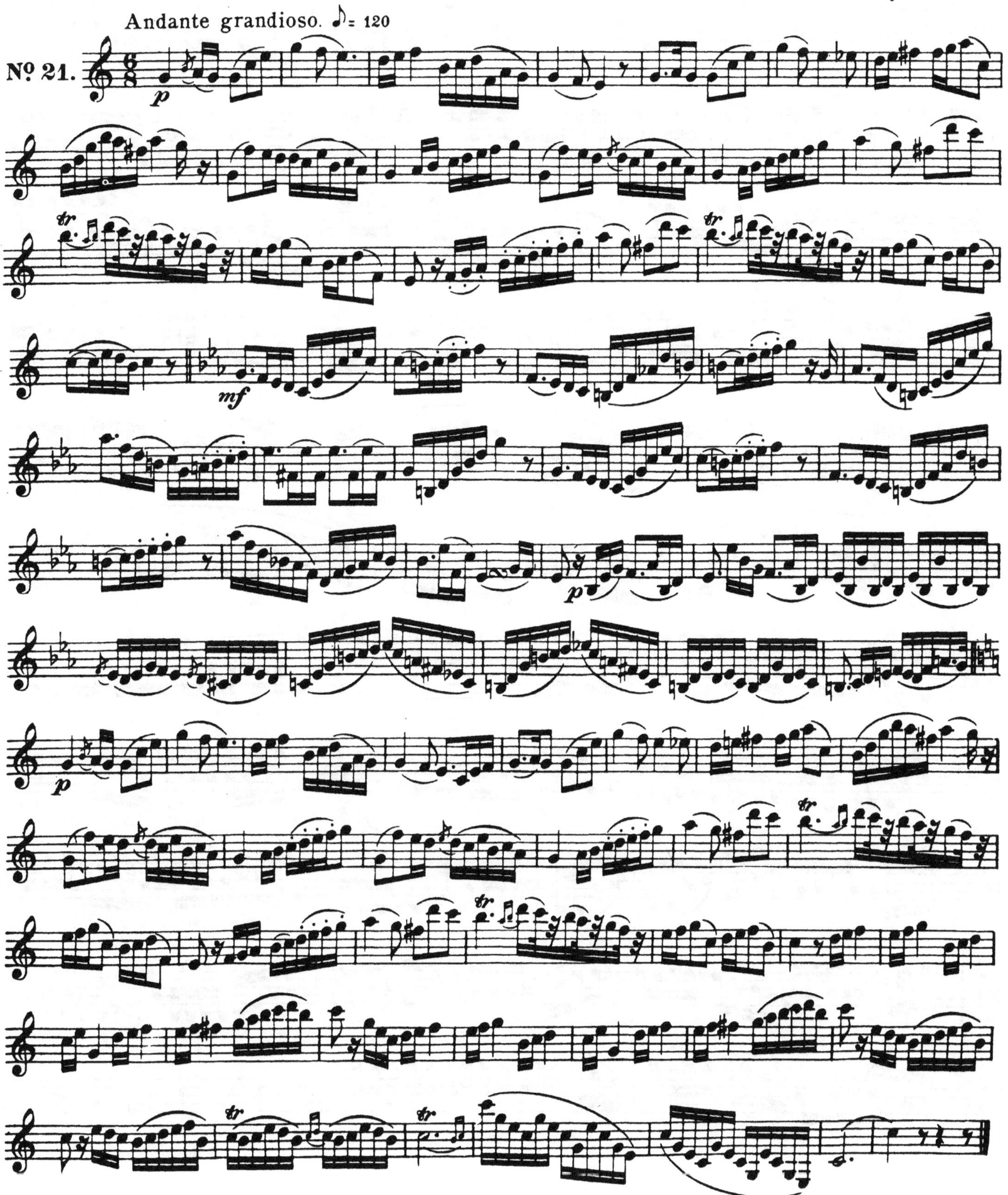

Allegro. 𝅗𝅥 = 112
Nº 22.
p

Allegro vivace. ♩. = 88
Nº 23.

Adagio. ♪ = 96
Nº 24.
f
dim.
p
cresc.
f
dim.
p
cresc.
cresc.
dim.
p
p
pp
mf
f et soutenu.
f
p
cresc.
f
dim.
p
p
pp
p
cresc.
f dim.
p
pp rit.
Tempo
cresc.
p
f
pp

Allegro. 𝅗𝅥 = 120
Nº 25.
mf
p
mf

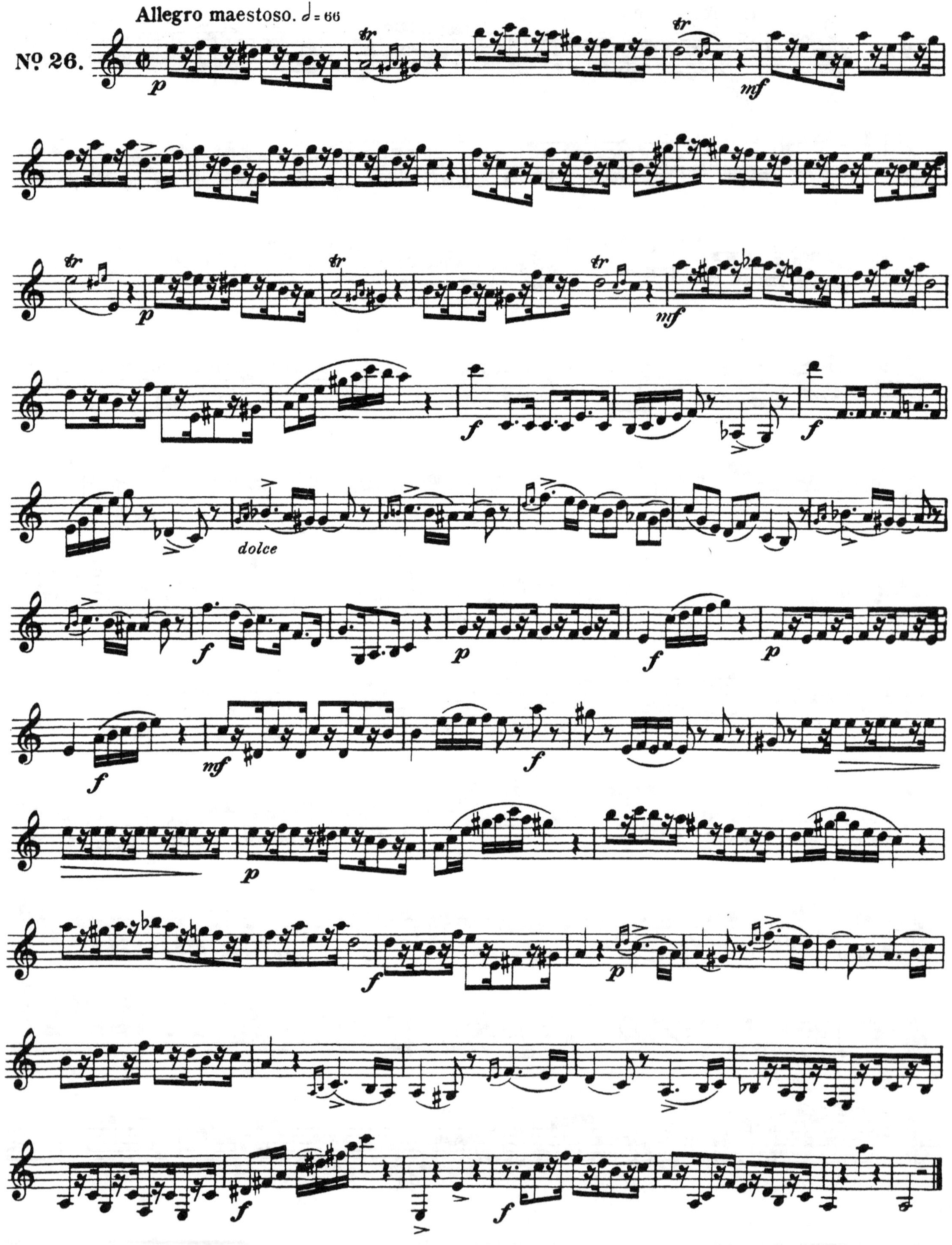

Allegro maestoso. 𝅗𝅥 = 66
Nº 26.
p
tr
mf
dolce
f

Nº 27.
Moderato. ♩= 96
♩= 104
p
pp
p

Moderato ♩ = 100
No. 28.
tr
sf
p
f

Moderato. 𝅗𝅥 = 100.
Nº 29.
p
mf
p
p
cresc.
f
p lento
a tempo
mf
f
f

Allegro moderato. 𝅗𝅥 = 112
Nº 30.
p
mf
tr

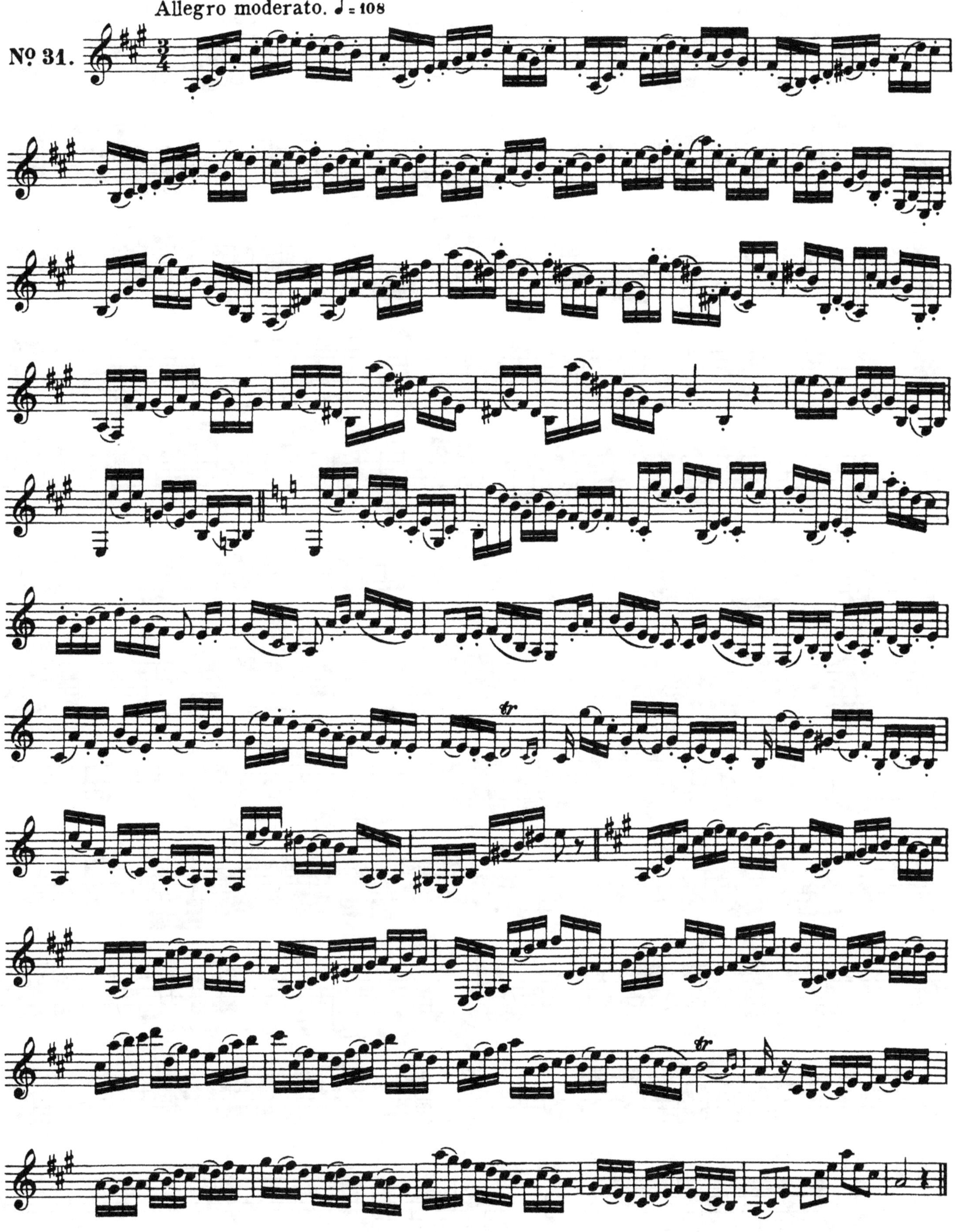
Allegro moderato. ♩= 108
Nº 31.
tr
tr

Adagio non troppo. ♩= 58
Nº 32.
mf
cresc.
f
p
dolce
tr
mf
p
dolce
f
p
cresc.
mf
cresc.
f
tr
p
mf con molto espress.
dim.
p
mf
riten.
dim. ppp
a tempo
p
p
agitato
cresc.
f
f et largement
cresc.
molto
f
molto espress.
rit.
p
a tempo
mf
f

Allegro moderato. 𝅗𝅥 = 108
Nº 33.
tr

Adagio. ♪ = 96
Nº 34.
dim.
cresc.
f
dim.
p
cresc.
dim.
p
cresc.
dim.
p
cresc.
dim.
ppp
cresc.
f
f
tr
cresc.
largement
f
dim.
rit.
3
Tempo.
p
mf e sostenuto
dim.
pp
p
mf
cresc.
f
dim. lento
p
morendo e rit.
très lentement.
ppp

Moderato. ♩= 112
Nº 35.
dolce.
tr
p
tr

Allegretto quasi Andante. ♩. = 63.
Nº 36.
tr
p lèger.
f
p
dim.

tr

Allegro. ♩= 112
Nº 37.
mf

Allegro vivace. ♩= 168
Nº 38.
f
p
pp
mf
dim.
ritard
a tempo
tr
fp
dim. poco rallent.

p
cre - - - - scen - - - do
f
p
mf

Allegro brillante. ♩= 112
Nº 39.
f
tr
mf
p
f
mf
dolce.
f

mf
tr
p
cresc.
f
tr

Allegro moderato. ♩= 108
Nº 40.
staccato

www.ingramcontent.com/pod-product-compliance
Lightning Source LLC
LaVergne TN
LVHW081423110826
845149LV00010B/1853

* 9 7 8 1 9 7 4 8 9 9 5 2 4 *